Blessings
& Prayers

for
New
Parents

Blessings & Prayers

for
New
Parents

Matthew J. Beck

Liguori
LIGUORI, MISSOURI

Imprimi Potest:
Harry Grile, CSsR, Provincial
Denver Province, The Redemptorists

Published by Liguori Publications
Liguori, Missouri 63057

To order, call 800-325-9521
www.liguori.org

Library of Congress Cataloging-in-Publication Data

Beck, Matthew J.
 Blessings and prayers for new parents / Matthew J. Beck.—First edition.
   pages cm
  ISBN 978-0-7648-2084-7
 1. Parents—Religious life. 2. Christian life. I. Title.
 BV4529.B43 2012
 242'.645—dc23

                                                            2011048674

Liguori Publications, a nonprofit corporation, is an apostolate of the Redemptorists. To learn more about the Redemptorists, visit Redemptorists.com.

Printed in the United States of America
16 15 14 13 12 / 5 4 3 2 1
First Edition

Table of Contents

Foreword

Christian parents are no different from any other parents with regard to the triumphs and difficulties all families face. However, my wife, Teresa, and I have often felt pressure to act in a certain way that is thought to be a "more Christian" way of living. In talking with other parents, we have discovered that many other Christian parents share our experience but don't know what to do to be a "true" Christian family.

Teresa and I believe authentic families of faith are those who open their hearts and homes to Christ and the Holy Spirit and who love their children with the love of God. Christian parents also strive to put virtues into practice, and by doing so, can often see fruits of the Spirit at work in their family. Most families, including Christian families, have their struggles. Even Mary and Joseph seemed to have times when they thought things could have gone better.

This short book is for imperfect parents who want to do their best at loving each other and raising healthy, happy, and holy kids. My hope is that parents will be able to pick it up and read a short section when they have a brief moment to relax, reflect, and pray, however infrequent that might be.

Because I have three daughters, I will sometimes write from the perspective of parents with daughters as that is my experience. The reflections, blessings, and prayers, however, can apply to any parent, family, son, or daughter.

May God bless you and your new family as you discover the joy and new love that await you.

CHAPTER 1

Anxiously Awaiting the Wonder

*Find your delight in the LORD
who will give you your heart's desire.*
PSALM 37:4

Teresa and I had been married for more than six years before I saw her eat a hot dog for the first time. She commented on *how much* she liked the taste of it. I did not need confirmation from a doctor or a store-bought test to know my wife was finally pregnant!

Teresa and I wanted to have children sooner, but it simply did not happen. By the time we were finally expecting, however, we thought we were prepared and were very excited that we would soon receive the gift of our own child.

We thank the Lord so much for answering our prayers. As soon as the doctor confirmed that Teresa was officially pregnant, we told everyone. I vividly remember the tears of joy and hugs shared with our closest friends who knew how much we wanted to have children. We could not believe we would be joining so many of our friends in becoming parents.

Our church community was also a blessing. Many parents knew the things we would need and gave us lots of diapers, wipes, diaper cream, blankets, and clothes. One woman knitted a quilt specifically for our child, even though we did not know one another very well. Being supported by so many people was very humbling and added much joy to the anticipation of the birth of our first child.

Growing in Virtue

The virtue of hope was necessary for us as new parents. We had waited for what seemed like an abnormally long time to conceive our first child. The temptation before Teresa became pregnant was to give in to despair. But clinging to hope kept us strong in faith. We prayed together for the Lord's will to be done in our lives.

We had lots of support, and one day someone prayed with us and proclaimed God had wonderful plans in store for us. She encouraged us to remain open to God's will and allow the Holy Spirit to move through our lives. Being a couple of hope during the time we were awaiting the arrival of our first child was our response to God's ongoing will for our lives.

A Blessing for the Woman With Morning Sickness

Morning sickness has begun
and the physical signs of pregnancy
are becoming more noticeable.

Lord, bless this woman with a peaceful spirit
beyond the physical challenges that come with pregnancy.

Pour the strength of your Holy Spirit into her.
When tiredness and nausea arise,
protect the child within her womb
and help her to focus on the joy that is yet to come.

We ask this through Christ, our Lord.
Amen.

A Prayer of Thanksgiving for a Pregnancy

Lord, you place the desire to be parents
into the hearts of married couples.

Thank you for the opportunity
to join in your creation through parenthood.

It is a wonder that life can come
from the love we share.
We ask your help—in all of this.

May the excitement we feel today
continue into the future.

We ask this through Christ, your Son.
Amen.

A Husband's Prayer for His Pregnant Wife

Lord, thank you for the beauty of my wife.
Thank you for the gift of her body
and its ability to sustain life
from the moment of the conception of our child
in her womb, through birth, and beyond.

Bless her with wholeness of mind,
body, and spirit throughout this pregnancy.

Give me the wisdom and strength
to support her throughout this journey.

I ask all of this through you.
Amen.

A Wife's Prayer for Her Husband

Lord, I married this man because he brings out the best in me.

Thank you for the gift that he is in my life.

As we begin the journey through parenthood,
help us to be united in your Spirit.

May the love we share with one another
and with our child be an example to others of your love.

I know there will be difficult and challenging times,
but help us to be patient and forgiving of each other.

Continue to guide him as my husband
and now build him up as a father too.

I ask this through you.
Amen.

Growing as a Parent

We had a friend over to our house one evening when Teresa was pregnant. After dinner, I was busy in the kitchen cleaning the dishes, but my work quickly escalated as I couldn't seem to stop. Our friend looked over to see me on top of the counters cleaning the shelves that were hardest to reach. She laughed and said, "Teresa, look at Matthew. He's nesting!"

The early stage of parenthood, before your child is born, is a great time to prepare the physical surroundings to where you will bring your baby home. It is also a good time to prepare your spiritual surroundings. If you're comfortable doing so, consider asking a church leader to bless your nursery. Or if it makes you more comfortable, invite your closest friends over and pray a simple prayer of blessing in the baby's room. You could also do this as a husband and wife if it suits you better. Your prayer might be:

....

Lord, fill our child's room with the peace of your Spirit. May our child rest peacefully and play cheerfully in this space. We ask this through Christ, our Lord. Amen.

Loving Your Child

When we first discovered we were pregnant, we were overwhelmed with a sense of joy. Take advantage of your joy and begin writing prayers of thanksgiving for the gift of your child in a journal. Think of the entries as letters to your child. You could then give the journal to your child at graduation, when he marries, or when she is expecting your first grandchild. Or just put it in a marked box and let your child find it one day.

CHAPTER 2

Holding
Your Newborn

*When she has given birth to a child,
she no longer remembers the pain because of her joy
that a child has been born into the world.*

JOHN 16:21

One of my favorite yearly activities is to set up our family's Nativity crèche right before Christmas. I have always sensed the deep love in the hearts of Mary and Joseph as they look upon their child, Jesus. I used to imagine what it would be like to be a new parent and gaze upon my own newborn child.

Well, it happened! My life was forever changed when our first daughter was born. No other experience in my life compares to holding our newborn daughter for the first time. The intense feelings were overwhelming as the nurse handed her to me wrapped in the delivery blanket. I realized this tiny baby was completely dependent upon my wife and me.

Teresa and I sobbed tears of joy. As I stood by my wife and held our daughter, we were so grateful that our prayers for a child had been answered. The doctor and nurses were crying too. It was a mystical moment, beyond complete understanding. All we could do was enter into it and receive God's grace. One of the nurses who was crying said, "It is such a blessing to be with a couple who are so happy to welcome their child." Teresa and I simply looked at each other and cried even harder.

I joked, "Please hand me another towel. I'm a bigger mess than anybody else here and I didn't even go through labor." I could not have been more grateful as I wiped my tears.

Fruit of the Spirit

The fruit of holding our child for the first time was peace. The overwhelming peace that came with God's grace at the moment of our first daughter's birth and the minutes afterward forever changed how Teresa and I defined our life together. We were no longer just a married couple; we were now parents. And in the first moments of living that out with our daughter in our arms and holding each other's hands, God's peace felt tangible in the delivery room. I think the doctor, nurses, and all those who entered sensed it too.

A Blessing for Your Newborn Daughter

Lord, you have given life to this child.
Now please pour your Spirit into her
and begin planting the seeds of faith deep within.

May she always know your unending love for her
and for all life as she grows
into the person you have created her to be.

We ask this through Christ, our Lord.
Amen.

A Blessing for Your Newborn's Bedroom

Lord, please bless this room with your loving presence.

When our child is at rest, give her happy dreams.

When she is at play, give her imagination.

Help her experience your loving presence always.

We ask this through Christ, our Lord.
Amen.

A Prayer for the First Moment of Parenthood

From this moment forward,
we are parents with new responsibilities.
Our child depends on our care.

Lord, help us to remember our love
for our child over and over as she grows,
especially when times are tough.

Thank you for the gift of our child.
Forever and forever.
Amen.

A Prayer for Families of Newborns as They Leave the Hospital

Lord, our new child is in her car seat,
and we are ready to take her home.

May this be the first of many safe
and wonderful journeys
that we take together as a family.

We are anxious as we face this new adventure.
Our home will never be the same.

May our child and those who visit
our home feel your presence
in how we live and love one another.

We pray this through Christ, our Lord.
Amen.

Growing as a Parent

Take advantage of your child's infancy to hold him or her often. Infants aren't very mobile, and their needs are basic. With all three of our children, the time went by way too fast for me.

Holding your infant can become a moment of prayer. As Christians we sometimes think a prayer needs to be lengthy to be meaningful, but that is incorrect. Sometimes the shortest prayers are best.

I remember holding our oldest daughter in the middle of the night a few days after she was born so Teresa could get a couple hours of solid rest. What a wonder it was to have this first miracle lie on my lap, simply stare at me, and smile. I was *very* tired, but I said a simple prayer for Teresa like, "Lord, multiply her sleep by ten so she feels rested when she awakens." Then I said a quick prayer for my new daughter and me that went something like, "God, help me remember this precious moment in the future when Julia and I aren't getting along." My daughter and I spent the remaining couple of hours simply staring at each other, repeating peaceful coos, in the darkness of the night.

Loving Your Child

It took work and the help of many wonderful people to welcome our first child into the world. We were at the hospital for fifteen hours before her birth. Afterward, everyone left the room, leaving Teresa, our baby, and me alone with our joy. We reveled in that moment as we took turns holding our child. As we listened to the soft cry of our newborn, we held hands and just enjoyed the grace of God we were experiencing. It was a moment of absolute serenity. Take some time and do the same.

CHAPTER 3

Doing Your Best as Parents

*Children's children are the crown of the elderly,
and the glory of children is their parentage.*

PROVERBS 17:6

After our first child was born, it seemed everyone who called had advice to share. Although voiced with love and concern, each family is unique, and not all advice offered is as helpful as intended.

Learning to be a parent is kind of like learning to be an athlete. A person can exercise, develop keen agility and balance, and read all about a specific sport, but until one actually participates in the sport, he cannot become an expert in that activity. Likewise, learning to be a good parent comes from actually doing it.

Teresa and I try to use our personal strengths to teach our children. Teresa is a strong reader. She began reading to our kids when they were very small. Now they read on their own before bed each night. I like to clean house and have tried to teach our children to take care of their things and clean their rooms, though I struggle to get them to make their beds most mornings. We have also found that being a good parent is about persevering, even when we don't feel like we are succeeding.

Parenting is about doing tasks that are not always enjoyable. We took a weekend vacation and stayed overnight at a resort hotel. I woke in the middle of the night to a gagging four-year-old and leaned over to help her, just as she vomited all over me and her bed. Teresa and I cleaned up the mess and helped our daughter get back to sleep. Many parenting experiences require us to step up and cope as best we can in the moment. Thus far, it has been an adventure filled with more experiences than we ever imagined!

Growing in Virtue

F aith-filled parents do not act haphazardly about what comes their way. If we did, it would put our families unnecessarily at risk. We practice the virtue of fortitude so that we can react reasonably to circumstances as they arise. With fortitude—also known as courage—we are able to be courageous parents whom our children will be able to trust and who in turn will know they are loved.

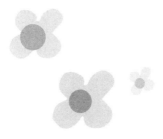

A Blessing for the Unknown Responsibilities of Parenthood

Loving God,
fill us with the power of your Spirit
as we journey through parenthood.

We do not know all that will happen along the way,
but help us have the faith and knowledge
that you are alongside us always—
especially in new and unexpected situations.

Give us the courage to forge ahead and do what is necessary
to be good parents as circumstances arise
and to trust that you will never give us more
than we can handle—with you.

We ask this through Christ, our Lord.
Amen.

A Prayer for Strength in Parenting

Lord, when we compare our family with others
who seem to be much more together than we are,
help us to remember that each family is unique.

Help us to recognize the gifts you have given us
and enable us to use those gifts to meet the challenges
of raising a family as they arise.

We ask this through you, who is Lord,
forever and ever.
Amen.

A Prayer for When Parents Make Mistakes

Lord, I love my child and want her to know it.
But sometimes I do a poor job of showing it
and I make mistakes.

Please forgive me, and help me forgive myself.
Help me learn from my mistakes
and become the parent you want me to be.

Thank you.
Amen.

Growing as a Parent

I have made mistakes. I guess even Christian parents aren't perfect. It would be easy to beat ourselves up for being imperfect, so it's important to recognize early on that mistakes can happen. The knowledge of our imperfection helps us turn to the Lord without shame as we look to God's grace. It also helps us to forgive ourselves and try to do better next time. I have had many opportunities to do a better job!

Loving Your Child

Think of one of your strongest personal gifts. Consider one way you can use that gift as a parent to help build your family during the next week. For example, if you are a swimmer, consider taking your family to a local pool and helping your child learn to enjoy swimming. Thank God for that gift in your life.

CHAPTER 4

Imperfect Yet Perfect Children

Train the young in the way they should go;
even when old, they will not swerve from it.

PROVERBS 22:6

I recently heard an adult refer to her child as "perfectly flawed." I think it was a fancy way of saying, "No one is perfect," even our children! It is inevitable that every parent and child will make mistakes, but that does not prevent us from deeply experiencing God's love in our families.

Teresa and I have discovered that each of our three daughters is unique. We often have specific hopes for them, but the challenge lies in letting them be who they truly are.

Our two oldest daughters, Julia and Maria, started taking piano lessons at the same time. It was clear after only a few months that Julia enjoyed it much more than Maria. So Maria stopped taking piano lessons and enrolled in an art class instead. She loved it!

We have found that it is important to recognize the personal gifts of each child. We knew from an early age that Maria was artistic. In her kindergarten class, each student was asked to draw a self-portrait about coming to school on the first day. The teacher hung the pictures for the parents to see when they came to parent night. I walked into the classroom to find other parents admiring the pictures and commenting on one in particular that stood out. It was extremely detailed, with a girl wearing a plaid dress, ponytails in her hair, and carrying a personally monogrammed lunch box. One dad asked, "Whose child drew that?" It was my daughter's picture, and it was amazing!

Growing in Virtue

Christian parents can love their children by practicing the virtue of justice, especially when it comes to loving multiple children. We have found that the goal is not to love one child more than another, but to love each child based on his or her personality and gifts. My wife and I performed an act of love when we supported Maria and her artistic skills by enrolling her in art camp and attending her art shows at the end. It was equally as loving when we encouraged Julia to pursue her love for music through band and piano lessons. We hope these concrete expressions of support will show them how much they are loved.

A Blessing for the Giftedness of Your Child

Christ came to bring us life.
Lord, now give us wisdom to help our children
live the life you have given them.

Help us to recognize their giftedness
and encourage them to develop their gifts as they grow.

Give us the wisdom to know the difference
between our desire for them and yours.
If these conflict, help us yield
to what is best for our child.

Help us to keep in mind that our kids are
your children who are placed into our care.

We ask this through Christ, our Lord.
Amen.

A Prayer for Imperfect Parents

We are created in the image of a God
who is perfect, yet we are not.

Despite our imperfections, help us to see
the goodness in each person,
especially in our family members.

May our imperfections give us humility
and help us take matters in stride as they arise.

Help us to know you are with us always.
Amen.

Growing as a Parent

Parenting is a gift in itself. God gives us life, and our children ultimately belong to God. Christian parents can be an example to other parents who might lack faith and hope.

When you see parents with children who are angry, tired, and stressed, say a simple prayer for them like, "Lord, fill those parents with your Spirit so that they may know your peace."

When you catch yourself neglecting your children as the gift that they are, you can pray, "God, please forgive me and help me to love my children more clearly through my actions and words."

Loving Your Child

Think of a gift your child possesses. Thank God for that gift in your child's life. Consider acknowledging that gift in your child. You might simply say something like, "Maria, you are a fantastic artist."

CHAPTER 5

Flexibility

Rejoice in hope, endure in affliction,
persevere in prayer.
ROMANS 12:12

I t is impossible for parents to anticipate or foresee every circumstance that might occur. Some things are simply beyond our control. Much of parenthood is learned through trial and error.

Recall the first time you flew with your children. If you haven't had this opportunity yourself, you may have seen other parents trying to go through security with small children, board the plane, get their entire family seated, and keep their children happy and quiet throughout the flight. Either way, you can probably imagine the high potential for something to go wrong with all that is involved with such a trip. A family can never fully prepare for what might happen in situations like this.

The key is to be flexible and ready to adjust plans when necessary. Many situations in life require moms and dads to step up and deal with the need at hand as best as they are able. Changing a dirty diaper in a crowded row of seats on an airplane during takeoff is not something any parent wants to do—but you do it because you love your child.

In the Gospel of Luke, we read about Mary and Joseph's returning home from Jerusalem. They thought their child, Jesus, had gone ahead of them, but after a day of walking, they realized Jesus was nowhere in their group. Can you imagine their panic? They probably asked themselves, "How could we have let this happen?" as they ran back to Jerusalem looking for him. You can only imagine their relief when they found him safe and sound, talking to the elders in the Temple. They probably had a good talking to him when they got home about not running off on his own!

Fruit of the Spirit

Seeking the gift of patience is something I need to do all the time, and my guess is that all parents can relate. When things do not go as smoothly as planned, I am often quick to react out of frustration and disappointment. I pray often for patience and the ability to respond calmly when the unexpected happens.

I have learned that patience is not simply received. Instead, it is a gift to develop within our lives through practice. Practicing patience can be rewarding in the long run. If Christian parents can't learn to be patient, we're going to be frustrated often!

A Blessing When Unexpected Circumstances Arise

May the Lord, who is all knowing,
send the peace of his Spirit into parents everywhere
so that they may trust that God is never distant.

We have shared in the act of creation
by becoming parents.
May God, our creator,
now strengthen us as we do what it takes
to raise our children.

We ask this through Christ, our Lord.
Amen.

Prayer for Flexibility (1)

Lord, we wish we knew all that is
about to come our way as parents.

We do our best to control matters and
get the results we think we want.
But the plans you have for us
are often much different than we imagine.

When things do not go as we anticipate,
help us to let go of our need to try to control everything.
Help us to trust in your plans and adjust our actions
according to whatever comes our way.

We pray this through Christ, our Lord.
Amen.

Prayer for Flexibility (2)

Lord, it is normal to be unprepared
throughout the journey of parenthood.

When surprises come our way,
give us your wisdom.

Help us to recognize what we can do,
what we cannot control,
and when to trust you more.

Thank you for the opportunity
to look back and laugh and learn
from anxiety and uncertainty.

We know now that you were present in those moments,
even if we were not able to recognize your presence.

Be with us always on the journey.
Amen.

Growing as a Parent

We had some old dining-room chairs we weren't using, so I put them by the window in our master bedroom, where I begin each day with a moment of silent meditation. The time can be short or it can last several minutes. I don't have a set rule of how to spend the time. I simply allow the Spirit to be present in the moment.

The time that I spend by the window each morning is critical to how my day goes. It helps me put each day into perspective and think about what is required of me to live as a modern-day disciple, with the primary vocation of being a husband and father. I believe the time I spend in the chair by the window allows the Spirit to seep into my life, give me strength, and guide me.

Christian parents need to have some kind of routine for personal prayer. The pitfall we often encounter is thinking there are rules for such prayer when it's actually a matter of finding what works for you. It's easy to overthink personal prayer. If you like to read, use Scripture or other reflections for your prayer. If you like music, listen to spiritual music. If you have ten minutes, that's great! It is not written anywhere that your personal prayer has to be sixty minutes a day. I realize it sounds like a cliché, but simply pray in the way you feel led by the Spirit.

Loving Your Child

Sometimes parenting can be stressful. On a good day, write a thank-you note to God on the back of a picture of your child. Then use it as a bookmark so you see it from time to time. It might read something like the following:

. . . .

Lord, thank you for my beautiful daughter. Please help her to be a happy child and know she is loved. Amen.

CHAPTER 6

Becoming a Family

Love is patient, love is kind.…Love never fails.

1 CORINTHIANS 13:4, 8A

B y the time people reach their late twenties, they have gone through a few transitions, such as puberty, leaving elementary school, entering middle school, graduating from high school, going to college, entering the military or attending a trade school, moving from one place to another, starting a job, and getting married.

When we were 28 and 29 years old, Teresa and I thought we had much of life figured out. We had both settled into steady and rewarding careers. We were about to celebrate our seventh wedding anniversary. What could possibly come our way that we were not prepared for? Any parent should be laughing at this point!

Our first daughter was born in August 2000. Our second arrived fifteen months later, and the third came in 2004. We have spent the last seven years trying to adapt and learn from the many high and low points that have come with being a family. It has been one of the most challenging and rewarding transitions of our lives, and the adventure seems to have no end in sight. We have transitioned from being two individuals to a married couple and now to becoming a family.

Love is the glue that holds our family together through all of the changes we have experienced. God continues to pour love into our lives, and we do our best to share that love with one another.

When we talk about our marriage and the journey toward becoming a family, Teresa and I often recall how God has been faithful to us. As we have sought him through prayer and meditation, a sincere peace has been planted within us that God's plan is unfolding through our life together and as our family grows.

Growing in Virtue

With the virtue of love comes charity. For Christian parents, this means giving our children what they need to be healthy. It also means setting aside personal interests to make family a priority in our lives. I used to enjoy downhill skiing, but to continue doing that now would mean spending too much time away from my family, so I don't go skiing. This is one way I have chosen to be charitable to my family. What is one way the Spirit may be calling you to be charitable toward your family?

Receive the Gifts of Parenting

Open your hearts and minds to be filled with the gifts of the Spirit:

Understanding

Peace of mind and heart that you and your children are loved by God, no matter what happens.

Counsel

Empowers parents to make the right choices for their family, most of the time.

Fortitude

Helps parents overcome their doubts and fears amid the chaos of a screaming child in a public place.

Knowledge

Parents find purpose and meaning in raising a family.

Piety

Fills us with the ability to see God in our children.

Awe and Wonder

Knowing that you are not in charge but that God is.

Growing as a Parent

A Catholic priest once challenged me to look at my life as a parent through the first three corporal works of mercy. It turns out the word *corporal* refers to the body, so these gave me new insights into how Christian parents are called to be modern-day disciples. The first and second corporal works are to feed the hungry and give drink to the thirsty. Our children would starve to death and die of dehydration if we didn't feed them and give them something to drink as infants. The third work is to clothe the naked. Each of our children had what we called "naked time" almost nightly when they were toddlers. I remember a night when one child threw a serious temper tantrum because she didn't want to wear her pajamas to bed. She shoved them under the closed bedroom door and fell asleep on the floor rather than do what we wanted.

Loving Your Child

Consider buying a medium-sized plastic bin for each child shortly after he or she is born. Write the child's name on it, then put it in your closet. As the child grows, put your favorite works of art, letters to Santa, pictures from school, and such things related to your child in the bin. It will provide you and your family many opportunities over the years to look through the memories and laugh and cry together.

We have done this for each of our children and occasionally find ourselves sitting on our bedroom floor browsing through the treasures with our children and talking and laughing about the memories.

CHAPTER 7

The Many Firsts

I have the strength for everything
through him who empowers me.
PHILIPPIANS 4:13

Have you ever received a call from a good friend after her child giggled for the first time? We experience great joy when we witness our child growing and learning new things. The many firsts that come with each child provide delightful moments of laughter and excitement.

When our second child took her first steps, I was out of town on business and sad to miss seeing her do so in person. Her walking for the first time was in the forefront of my thoughts throughout the trip. It is common for parents to be ready with a camera to capture the giggles, crawling, and steps on video. We are quick to e-mail the pictures and videos to our friends and post them for all to see—we are so proud of that first moment and assume everyone else will be too!

One of my favorite events is to witness the first time parents bring their newborn child to Mass. You can see the nervousness, excitement, and wonderment of new parents. They are wondering, "Will our child cry throughout the Mass or remain asleep?" What they don't know is that an infant who cannot talk or walk is actually quite simple to have at Mass, especially compared to a toddler!

As we experienced the many firsts that come with being new parents, we found ourselves having to quickly learn how to adapt to the changes within our family over and over again. Now we realize that no matter how many firsts occur, so many more will come that we cannot begin to imagine them all.

I am filled with the hope of seeing our first child graduate from high school, begin her career, and bring home a boy to meet her parents. These first experiences with our children are moments to cherish, even when they are difficult. All of them have enabled me to see the beauty of God's creation growing right before my eyes.

....

Thank you, Lord, for the many firsts that come with parenthood. May I never grow tired of experiencing them. When a "first" parenting experience comes my way, may I draw strength from your Holy Spirit in the face of challenges. May I be filled with joy when they bring laughter. May I be filled with inspiration when surprises come my way.

Fruit of the Spirit

The fruit of joy floods the lives of Christian parents as we witness children giggle, sit up, crawl, or walk for the first time. With lives of faith, these become moments filled with God's grace, where we are moved to thank our Lord for the gifts of our children.

A Blessing for the Firsts in Parenthood

With happiness my child coos, giggles, and eventually laughs.
Lord, may the many firsts in the life of my children fill me
with the newness of life that your Spirit brings into this world.

It is by that grace that we have been created.
May that grace now fill us. May we become a first for others
who long to experience your love in this world.

Bless us as we share your grace with others
through choosing to reach out to them in love and peace.

We ask this through Christ, our Lord.
Amen.

A Prayer for Openness and Strength

Lord, help me to enjoy the anticipated and unexpected
first experiences that will come as my child grows up.

Help me remember that you are also rejoicing
as she crawls for the first time, giggles for the first time,
and calls me "daddy" for the first time.

May the joy that fills my heart in those moments
be a reminder of your joy for all your children.

May it remind me that I am your child
and that you love me,
just as I love my daughter.
May it change me and help me have
a joy-filled spirit that I share with others.

I pray this through Christ, my Lord.
Amen.

Growing as a Parent

If someone had to choose one word to describe you as a parent, what would you want it to be?

I hope others look at me and see a joyful person. My wife and kids refer to me as "grumpy daddy" some days, so I realize I am not always joyful. But I think deep down they know I am filled with joy, and I think joy helps them know that life is precious and that they are cherished.

Christian parents may find it helpful to identify a Fruit of the Spirit that is most often manifested in their lives. Working daily to give witness to that gift should be of help in living a holy life.

Loving Your Child

New parents simply need to be ready. You are not going to be able to catch every moment on film or video, but you will get many of them. If you are a new parent, ask God to fill you with expectant faith, to experience grace in the many firsts to come as your child grows.

If you have been a parent for a while, think of one moment when your child surprised you with something new. Thank God for the joy of that moment. Tell your child of the joy it brought to your life when it happened.

CHAPTER 8

Expanding the Safety Zone

Trust in the LORD with all your heart.

PROVERBS 3:5

Before I became a parent, I used to brag about how my children were going to be downhill skiers by the time they were three years old. I was going to be an active parent who got my kids out into the world, experiencing all types of new adventures. Boy, was I wrong!

When we brought our first child home from the hospital, we were excited to show her to all our family and friends. I was particularly excited to take her to church. Like most first-time parents, at the first inklings of crying, I took our daughter out to the foyer, worried that the crying would disturb those around us. A woman immediately walked up to me, swooped Julia out of my arms, and began talking and singing to her. She stopped crying, and the woman said to me, "The baby can sense that you are nervous. You have to be more confident and assure her that everything will be OK." My ego was crushed!

To be truthful, I was filled with doubts and insecurities. I wondered if my child would ever feel safe with me or if I could protect her if something happened unexpectedly. I quickly became more comfortable staying at home with my daughter than venturing out into new territory.

Eventually, I realized it's not good to live in fear, so I began taking small steps. Going to the homes of a few friends was one of the early steps. Going to church also felt safe. All new parents will have to discover what feels safe to them. I still have not taken my kids downhill skiing, but we take family vacations and have even traveled to Disneyland and Hawaii. I don't know if my insecurities about protecting my children will ever disappear, but I hope they prepare me for the real emergencies that may one day come our way.

It must have required quite a bit of trust in the Lord for Joseph and Mary to respond to the angel of the Lord and flee to Egypt after the visit from the Magi. Clearly, they wanted to protect their child, Jesus, from Herod's soldiers. I'm sure going to an unfamiliar place with their newborn would have made them a bit nervous. I find comfort in this story amid my fears and anxieties.

Growing in Virtue

Christian parents exercise prudence when they decide the timing is right for something for their children and family. What might be right for one family may not be right for another. For example, if most members of the family aren't athletic with risk-taking personalities, I am not going to spend a family vacation at a ski resort. But that might perfectly fit someone else's family. And that's OK.

I turn to the Lord almost daily and ask for the Spirit's help in making the right decisions for my family. This is for the sake of their health, safety, and happiness. I wish I could say I always make the right choices, but I don't. So the flip side of this virtue is forgiving ourselves when we fail and moving ahead with the intention of doing better.

A Blessing for Nervous Parents

Lord, our newborn children are completely
dependent on our care. Please pour your Spirit
of peace into our lives as parents.

Help us to adjust accordingly as
change comes quickly into our lives
with the birth of each child.

Bless us as we take small steps forward
to increase our comfort zone with our children.
Increase our confidence with each step.

We ask this through Christ, our Lord.
Amen.

A Prayer as the New Adventures Begin

Lord, we have many hopes and dreams
for the activities we will be able to do with our children.
Help us to remember that your plan for our family
includes many times of fun and laughter.

Thank you for the many good adventures
we will have together, whatever they may be.

We pray this through Christ, our Lord.
Amen.

A Prayer When Things Go Wrong

Bad things happen that we don't always understand.
Help us find you in our disappointment and tears.
Help us believe that you also weep amidst our pain and anger.

Pour your healing Spirit upon our pain,
and bring us wholeness and peace.

Help us to trust in you,
even when it is difficult to understand
what is happening around us and to us.

We ask this through Christ, our Lord.
Amen.

Growing as a Parent

I have a make-believe list of things I never want to do in life. On that list are things like skydiving, bungee jumping, and riding in a hot-air balloon. Some people love such adventures, but not me. Although parenting often stretches us further than we expect, I think my list would have been a lot longer if I'd known the challenges I would face as a parent. I don't regret all the stresses and thrills of parenthood, but I'm glad I didn't know what they were, because I might not have taken the risk. Even the best parents can't predict what will happen in their families. Instead, we approach each day as a gift and try to live it, filled with God's Spirit and surrounded by God's grace. That is a risk well worth taking.

Loving Your Child

No one knows your child better than you do. Try to pray a one-sentence prayer each morning for the wisdom of the Spirit as you consider what is best for your children. It might be something like this:

....

Lord, grant me the wisdom of your Spirit today to make decisions that are best for my child.

CHAPTER 9

God and Toddlers

*And whoever receives one child such as this
in my name receives me.*

MATTHEW 18:5

Have you ever walked through a grocery store and heard a two-year-old crying in the next aisle? All parents hope that will never be their child. Good luck with avoiding that! Toddlers are some of the most unpredictable creatures on earth. Their bodies become functional while their minds are still developing.

One of our daughters was potty training and ran into the grocery store ahead of my wife, proceeded to pull down her pants, and go on the floor of the store. Now, Teresa was happy that our daughter did not wet her pants, but she was overcome by shock with what *our* child was doing in the store.

Our third daughter's nickname is "Monkey." She inherited that name because she liked to take risks and climb furniture. I vividly recall finding her standing on the dining-room table and reaching for the chandelier. Yikes! My risk-taker was a toddler!

Realizing that toddlers are active and ready to explore the world immediately around them is the key to living with them. Our responsibility as parents is to do our best to protect them from the things we can anticipate might happen. Then we have to learn from the times we fail.

Finally, we have to laugh at toddlers. They are hilarious in many ways. One time Julia thought she was being funny as she ran down the hallway with her blanket over her head. It *was* funny until she ran into the wall. She wasn't hurt, but she quickly learned not to try that trick again!

Growing in Virtue

Parenting a toddler requires many different virtues, but if I have to pick one to exercise most often, it is reasonable restraint. Most of us have been at church when a toddler is present. Isn't it awesome when they speak out of turn and loudly say "Amen"? We could get upset and scold them, but it would make more sense to praise the child for participating. Such a choice as a parent will encourage the child to continue to make an effort to participate in the service. Perhaps next time the child's timing will be a little better!

A Blessing for Parents and Toddlers

Lord, we thank you for the gift of our child.

Now that she is a toddler,
please protect her as she begins to explore new things.

Give us the knowledge
to help foresee circumstances
that may arise and put her at risk.

Help us to prepare for the many challenges
that will come our way as she grows.
Bless us with patience and laughter.

We ask this through Christ, our Lord.
Amen.

A Prayer for Toddlers

Lord, may we treat our toddler with dignity
and follow her example
of being open to love and learning.
We pray this through Christ, our Lord.
Amen.

Growing as a Parent

A teen once referred to me as the oldest kid he knows. What a wonderful compliment! Christian parents should try not to be too serious all the time. There are lots of things to laugh at, and toddlers should bring lots of laughter to our lives. Although I laughed a lot when my own children were toddlers, I wish I'd been more relaxed and laughed a bit more often.

It can be difficult to sit back as a parent and watch our children grow from tiny little children into young boys and girls, but it happens, no matter how much we worry.

Loving Your Child

If your child is not yet a toddler, be ready to capture some silly moments on video by keeping the camera handy. There are going to be many moments you will want to remember and show your child when he or she is older! If your child is older, take a few moments to sit together as a family and watch family videos or look through family photos of when your children were toddlers. Laugh together as you recall the memories!

CHAPTER 10

Growing in Mind and Body

Therefore, let us leave behind the basic teaching about Christ and advance to maturity.

HEBREWS 6:1

It is rewarding to watch our children grow. When my oldest daughter was around seven years of age, I walked by her bedroom and heard music. I peeked through the partially open door and saw her dancing and singing. At that moment I realized she was no longer the baby or toddler I once knew. She was becoming a young girl with feelings, a sense of humor, and the ability to reason for herself.

I have to admit that a part of me was relieved with this change. As our children grow older, they become less dependent on us in many ways. I imagine all parents feel some sense of relief the first time they leave the house without a diaper bag! At the same time we experience a bit of sadness that the months and years go by so quickly.

As our children have grown, Teresa and I have had to grow as parents as well. We have made many of the same sacrifices, choices, and mistakes other parents have made, but in all cases, moving ahead has been the key. It's fascinating to realize that as our children mature, so do we. Yet maturity is not a goal we eventually reach or achieve. Sometimes maturity comes from recognizing our need to ask for help. I also have to recognize the immaturity of my children and have realistic expectations for them. Immaturity isn't a bad thing, it is simply a reality. Sometimes I might be too immature to analyze or understand a situation; I simply have to deal with it! My ability to deal more confidently with different situations that occur will grow with each experience as our children grow—and as Teresa and I grow as parents.

Fruit of the Spirit

Gentleness can be seen in the house when Christian parents choose to love their children.

Our family is quite loud, and I'm the loudest among the five of us. I've got a strong voice and have always spoken loudly, especially when I'm excited about something. So most days I don't sound very gentle. However, I hope my gentleness shows through my loudness by the words I choose to speak, by the hugs I give my children, and by the smiles I give them across the room.

A Blessing for Your Growing Family

We were once a married couple,
and now we have children.
Lord, as our family grows,
please continue to pour your blessings into our home.

May your peace reside where we live,
and may we treat one another with love.

When we make bad choices and fail to love,
help us to ask for forgiveness and healing
and forge ahead to do better next time.

May we open our home to the presence of
your Holy Spirit today and in the future.
May your Spirit build and sustain our family.

We ask this through Christ, our Lord.
Amen.

A Prayer for Growth

Lord, we cannot stop time and go backward.
Help us continue to move ahead,
sharing your love with one another
and with each child as our family grows.

We look forward to the many moments
we will continue to share as a family.
Sometimes we will laugh.
Sometimes we will cry.

Help us to grow in knowledge
and understanding with each experience.

We commit ourselves to
lifelong learning to all that
you have planned for our family.
Amen.

Growing as a Parent

Christian parents are not perfect. Perfection is not our goal. Our goal is to grow in faith and knowledge while our children grow. Our ongoing religious education as adults should be even more important to us than that of our children. How can we pass on faith and knowledge to our children if we are not engaged in lifelong learning and personal growth ourselves?

Loving Your Child

Think of how your children best know they are loved. One might like to be hugged, while it might be important for another child to hear you speak loving words. Share your love in whatever way your children perceive they are loved.

Our youngest daughter likes to help with little chores around the house to show her love for her mom and me. One morning I made her bed for her and got the pillow she really likes when she went to bed at the end of the day. It might seem simple, but the little ways in which we show our love for our children help them have a well-rounded experience of being loved.

CHAPTER 11

Letting Go

When you call me, and come and pray to me,
I will listen to you. When you look for me,
you will find me.

JEREMIAH 29:12–13

Taking our oldest child to the first day of kindergarten was, perhaps, the most bittersweet moment of my life. The child who depended on me for her safety and well-being was going to be in the care of someone else. I'd left her with a baby-sitter before, but there was something psychologically different about leaving her at school for the first time.

Teresa and I walked with Julia to the classroom, helped her find her seat, and then left. We held hands and cried as we walked down the hallway and out the doors of the school. There was a sign in the hallway that read, "Cookies and punch for first-timers," but we didn't want others to see us crying. Our second child ran to the classroom on her first day of kindergarten. We put our third child on the bus for her first day. It got easier with each child, but it was still a moment of letting go and trusting that our child was safe with other adults in charge.

Since then, there have been many times of having to let go with a sense of uncertainty: letting go of the need to walk with my daughter when she goes to a friend's house; letting go of helping her choose what to wear and helping her get dressed in the morning; letting go of holding my little child in my arms as she sleeps during Mass. Our letting go as parents has helped each of our children grow and has forced us to turn to the Lord, praying that the Spirit look after our children as they venture onward.

Scripture doesn't tell us anything about Jesus' first day of school, but circumstances surely would have required Joseph and Mary to let go of their fear, anxiety, and uncertainty as spouses and parents. Mary had to let go to say yes to giving birth to Jesus. Joseph had to let go to marry a pregnant woman. Imagine how Mary must have had to let go as Jesus began his ministry for which he eventually gave his life.

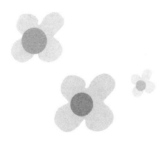

Growing in Virtue

Christian parents demonstrate proper concern for their children. Although concern isn't listed as an official virtue, it is a virtuous habit to practice. We put our children in car seats, cover electrical outlets, and install drawer locks for their safety. The struggle for me is discerning the difference between proper concern and overprotection. For my children to be happy and holy, I think having the opportunities to make mistakes, learn from them, and grow from them are important. For me, the challenge is to identify and prevent the mistakes that may cause serious harm.

A Blessing for Parents as We Let Go

As my child grows and becomes the person
you are calling her to be,
bless me as I let go—please.

Help me see how my role
as a parent only changes.
Fill me with assurance
that I will always be my girl's daddy.

When times are tough
and I miss the way things used to be,
help me to remember she is your child too.

May your hopes for her be fulfilled,
and may I rejoice as I get to see that happen.

I ask this through Christ, my Lord.
Amen.

A Prayer for Letting Go

Joseph and Mary had to let go of their
uncertainties and fears as spouses and parents.
Lord, help us follow their example
and let go of our fears.

Give us the wisdom
to recognize when our children
are ready to try things on their own.
Help us to rejoice when they succeed
in taking the right actions
and making correct decisions.

Help us give our anxieties to you
from time to time and trust
that you will watch over our children as they grow.

We pray this through Christ, our Lord.
Amen.

Growing as a Parent

A close friend of mine is a parent of young adults. He often reminds me that Christian parents are constantly learning how to give their children room to make mistakes. Children need the opportunity to learn from their mistakes. He says that the temptation for all parents is to jump in and prevent the mistake. He encouraged me to do all I can to help my children do their best, then sit back and be prepared to help them correct their mistakes and learn from them. I found it to be pretty good advice, although it is still hard to let go and let them learn on their own.

Loving Your Child

Spend time around the dinner table recalling what the first day of school was like for you and your child. Laugh about it. Cry about it. Thank God for those feelings and memories. You can do this at the beginning of each new school year and share the meaning each year brings.

CHAPTER 12

Pain Cannot Be Prevented

He will wipe every tear from their eyes, and there shall be no
more death or mourning, wailing or pain,
[for] the old order has passed away.

REVELATION 21:4

While we adults were inside having a relaxing conversation, our children were outside, running and playing. Then a crying child was heard and seen running toward the house with her hand over her eye. It was Maria! A tree branch had struck her in the eye during their games.

Teresa decided to take her to the emergency room to have a doctor look at it. She stepped up as any good parent should and dealt appropriately with the situation. Thankfully, it was a minor injury that required antibiotic drops and eye cream for the next few days while the scratch on the eyeball healed. I was not as calm as Teresa. The waiting while they were at the hospital for a couple of hours was physically and emotionally painful for me. No parent wants to think of or see his child in pain.

When the reality struck me that my daughter had suffered harm, my mind began asking, "What if?" What if I had told her not to run through the woods? What if I had trimmed those trees? What if the injury is serious? Of course, now I realize the "what ifs" were pointless worries. I also know pain is a part of life. Thanks be to God my child's first visit to the emergency room was not too serious.

When I think of how Jesus died, it's hard to imagine the pain Mary must have felt when she witnessed her son being scourged, spit upon, nailed to the cross, and killed. If I had to witness my child in that kind of agony and pain, I don't think I could ever fully recover emotionally.

One of the most painful experiences of my life thus far was receiving a phone call from a friend telling me that his son had just died in his crib during his nap. My friend was in so much pain he could barely speak. Since then, we have occasionally shared some brief conversations with our friends about their son. I am filled with a sense of hope as I see them loving their children who are still alive and sharing laughter together. They have shown me how parents can have hope and happiness even after such pain.

Growing in Virtue

The virtue of fortitude is necessary when we have to take our children to the emergency room. Fortitude gives us the strength to stand strong through the challenges that come our way, especially the ones that involve the well-being of our children.

A few years ago I heard of the tragic incident of a young girl who fell from the edge of a cliff. Her dad immediately jumped over the cliff's edge in an effort to save her, and he suffered serious injury. This example shows how the virtue of fortitude is put into practice. Parents will do whatever they can to protect their children from physical harm.

A Blessing When Your Child Is in the Emergency Room

Lord, you breathed life into my child at her conception.
Now breathe that same life into her wounded body.

Bless her nurses and doctors with wisdom.
Help them do all they can to help her.

Please bless us too as we stand by her side at this time.
May the love we demonstrate strengthen her spirit.

We ask this through Christ, our Lord.
Amen.

A Prayer of Protection for Your Child

In the name of Jesus, by the power of your Spirit,
I ask that you protect my child from any harm today.
Watch over her and guide all who are part
of decisions that will keep her safe and well.

I pray this through Christ, my Lord.
Amen.

Growing as a Parent

Pain seems to be a fact of life and sometimes unavoidable. It is difficult to teach our children how to deal with pain because it is such a reality. Since my children were very young I have tried to speak honestly about pain that comes with living.

One day we had to have our nine-year-old orange tabby cat, Mike, put to sleep. Our entire family was there with him as he was injected with the final shot. We cried. We petted him. We told him we loved him. And we prayed.

To grow as strong Christian parents, we simply need to pray for the strength to deal with pain when it arises. I also think the love we share can overcome the pain. We shared lots of hugs and kisses in our home after saying good-bye to Mike. It's important that our children learn that there is life after pain.

Loving Your Child

If your child has never been seriously injured, give thanks to God at this moment. If something has happened to your child that you wish you could have prevented, say a prayer to forgive yourself. Ask the Lord to fill your heart with a sense of trust in his care and concern for you and your child. Your prayer may be something like this:

....

God, I thought things would be different and I've made mistakes. Please forgive me, and help me to trust in your plan for my life and the lives of everyone in my family. Amen.

CHAPTER 13

A Growing Family—
Every Child Matters

Your wife will be like a fruitful vine within your home,
your children like young olive plants around your table.

PSALM 128:3

The birth of each child into the family opens new doors of opportunities and possibilities for your home. The questions I asked myself were, "How am I going to help each of these children know he or she is loved as much as their other siblings?" and "What can I do to make each child know she is unique and special?"

One tradition I've practiced is to take each of my daughters out for lunch on her birthday at a place of her choosing. Each child is a true gift from God. This time just between the two of us makes them feel extra special. It makes me feel really special too to have the opportunity to spend this individual time with each of them.

One thing that helped calm my concern that each child feel special was to realize that each one is genuinely unique from his or her siblings. As would be expected, they have some similarities, but they have just as many striking differences. Teresa and I work to recognize each child's uniqueness. We praise our daughters for their unique gifts and help them explore what they like and dislike, which helps them discover their unique talents.

One of our oldest daughter's assignments in school a few years ago was to write some sentences beginning with "I am" that describe her. The first sentence she wrote was, "I am beautiful." What a grace. I believe the Lord is at work in our family and in her life helping her to have such confidence.

I don't always succeed in making each child feel special, but I intend to continue making it a priority to help each of my daughters know how beautiful, unique, and special each one is in the eyes of our Lord—and in the eyes of her parents!

Fruit of the Spirit

L ove is a gift poured out by God. As Christian parents, we should seek it out daily in our prayers. Take a moment right now to pray, "Lord, open my heart to receive your love." When we receive the Lord's love, we can in turn share it with our children. We demonstrate our love for our children through our words, actions, and thoughts.

A Blessing for Limitless Love

Lord, your love is limitless.
May parents know they can
offer love without limits as well.

Please pour your love into the
lives of parents everywhere
so that we may be able
to help our children
know of your love for them.

When they become parents one day,
may our children in turn love their children
from the love you pour into their lives.

We ask this through Christ, our Lord.
Amen.

A Prayer for Oneness

Lord, you create all of your children
out of love, and each one of us is unique.
We have different likes, dislikes, and talents.
Help me to remember that each child of mine is unique.
No one is exactly quite like her.

May our family learn to recognize
the differences between us
and celebrate each person's gifts.
Help us to recognize how your Spirit
unites us in faith as one family
in all our uniqueness.

We pray this through Christ, our Lord.
Amen.

Growing as a Parent

I like to think of *love* as a verb. We either choose to love or we choose not to love.

God pours love into creation without limits. For me, God's love comes in the ordinary occurrences of family life, such as sitting around the dinner table, sharing a phone conversation with my wife in the middle of the day, talking with my parents who live far away, or spending a moment in silent prayer each morning.

When we allow God's love to enter our lives, it changes us. I need more and more of it. The change for me hasn't been a one-time thing. I'm a work in progress!

May we continue to be families filled with the love of God and share it with those who are most in need of experiencing that love, especially our children.

Loving Your Child

Go into your child's bedroom after she is asleep tonight or stand by the doorway if you're worried about waking her. If possible, kneel or stand at the foot of her bed and listen to her breathe as she sleeps. Silently thank God for the gift of life within her. Your prayer might be something like, *Lord, thank you for my daughter (son).*

CHAPTER 14

Discovering Family Time— What Works for You?

*They devoted themselves to the
teaching of the apostles and to the communal life,
to the breaking of the bread and to the prayers.*

ACTS 2:42

I believe that God creates families to provide windows so others can see examples of God's love for all people. One day a person might look through a window into our home and see a place filled with laughter; another day a person might see a home filled with anger and frustration. There is no one specific way to live as a good Christian family, but we have found some helpful principles that might be applied in all families.

First, we have found it important to spend quality time together each day. It may be taking a short walk with our dogs, sitting around a campfire, or eating a bowl of ice cream together. Our family recently began a small hobby farm with chickens. I often wonder what we did before we had chickens because they have provided countless moments of family time.

Dinnertime is probably the most important hour of each day for us. There is something very powerful about sitting around the same table and sharing a meal together. For Teresa and me, the value is not in the food, but in the coming together as a family.

We have also done our best to be connected with a vibrant faith community. Being supported in prayer by members of our church is powerful. We also take trips together. It is awesome to see my children laughing and playing in a setting apart from the routine of everyday life. Personal prayer is also crucial to quality family time. I do not feel whole as a spouse or as a parent when I fail to spend some part of my day in personal prayer. I encourage all parents to find a practice of personal prayer that builds and sustains them as they in turn try to build their family in faith.

Growing in Virtue

Time is not an official Christian virtue, but how we use it should be a practiced virtue of Christian parents. The way we use our time demonstrates our priorities. Dedicating time to be with our family is crucial to growing in health and holiness. When we choose to spend time with our family sitting around the dinner table instead of in our offices, it lets our children know they matter. As they grow older, I hope our children will discover that the little choices we make can have a huge impact on the world around us.

A Blessing for Family Time

Lord, you have brought us together as a family.
Bless us as we spend time
enjoying one another's company.

Fill our family with the same Spirit
that graced Mary and Joseph
on the night Christ was born
and when they returned to find him
in the Temple teaching the elders.

May our times together as a family
be blessed with many wonders.

Help us to be committed to our family
by spending quality time together—often.

We ask this through Christ, our Lord.
Amen.

A Prayer for Family Time

Bless our family with creativity.
May we find new ways to enjoy
one another's company and
grow together as your children.

Fill our home with love and grace
so that others will look into the window of our home
and see you present within us.
May our time together be an example
of your love for all people.

We pray this through Christ, our Lord.
Amen.

Growing as a Parent

I often hear older parents say that children grow up too fast. I now realize parenthood is an ongoing transition that will never end. It is not a task that I will develop a long-term routine for, but a responsibility I must strive to do well on a daily basis. I can't predict exactly how each stage of parenthood will go and how many mistakes I will make.

Christian parents strive to recognize the Holy Spirit moving in their families. We don't always know what the actions of the Spirit will be, but my hope as a Christian parent is that we will be flexible and virtuous and do our best to be loving and prayerful. I hope we will always be charitable with our time and spend it abundantly with our family.

Loving Your Child

Ponder how your family enjoys spending time together. Ask your spouse, "What do you think are the most important ways our family spends time together?"

Thank the Lord for your spouse and for your children with a simple prayer such as:

....

Thank you, Lord, for my wife and kids. Help me be a holy parent. May the time we spend together build the love between us and help us grow. Help me value family time and strive to keep it a priority.

Conclusion

I kneel before the Father, from whom every family
in heaven and on earth is named.
EPHESIANS 3:14–15

Husbands and wives marry and strive to love each other. We bear children, who come from the love we share. God has given us the privilege of sharing in creation when we open our marriages to bringing forth the life of a child.

I think parents today often feel alienated from other people and the whirlwind of activities happening all around us while we are at home feeding our children or caring for a sick child. It is easy to think we might be missing out on something; however, one of the greatest gifts in our lives is sitting right before us.

Many activities in life begin and end, such as high school, college, or a job. But parenthood is an activity that has no end. Once we become parents, we will never be the same. The challenge for us is to be engaged in our role as parents. What that looks like is going to be different for each of us.

Let us rejoice in the gifts of God's grace that come as our families spend time together. Let us be open to loving our children and to forgiving ourselves when we fall short. Let us press ahead as we work to build healthy, happy, and holy families. God will be with us all along the way.

Sharing the Faith With Your Child
From Birth to Age Four
ISBN: 9780764-815232

With practical wisdom the authors of this handbook show parents how their daily lives, experiences, and relationships reinforce their role as parents. The book includes chapters on: Parenting, Being a Family, Being a Catholic Family, and Rearing Children in a Christian Family.

Handbook for Today's Catholic Children
ISBN: 9780764-810138

Written for younger children, *Handbook for Today's Catholic Children* presents basic tenets of the Catholic faith in terms they can understand. Chapter topics include "All About Sin—More About Love," and "The Church Cares for You," which discusses the Ten Commandments. Each chapter ends with a short prayer.

Saints on Call
Everyday Devotions for Moms
ISBN: 9780764-820342

Christine Gibson's *Saints on Call* will help mothers in every walk of life to pray and reflect on the opportunities for holiness found in daily life. Designed with the on-the-go mom in mind--and featuring over 50 reflections—this book is helpfully categorized by a mother's daily situations and struggles.